Decorating with AUSTRALIAN FEDERATION
STAINED GLASS

JILLIAN SAWYER

Photography
CHRIS GARNETT

Published by
GLASS BOOKS PTY LTD

Printed in Western Australia

*For two of the most important people in my life,
Bet and Des Carlson, my mum and dad.*

For their kind co-operation in the photography of their homes, our sincere thanks to:

*Mr & Mrs Hollingsworth
Mr & Mrs McOnie
Mr & Mrs Negoescu
Mr & Mrs Pantall
Mr & Mrs Strautins
Mr & Mrs Sutton*

Published by Glass Books Pty Ltd
PO Box 891 Subiaco Western Australia 6904
sales@glassbooks.com.au
www.glassbooks.com.au

August 1994
Reprinted February 1995
Reprinted March 1996
Reprinted October 1997
Reprinted December 1999
Reprinted August 2002

Foreword

The fervour of Australian nationalism erupted with the federation of Australia as a nation in 1901 and saw the birth of the first distinctively Australian house style - THE FEDERATION HOUSE.

With its open verandahs and relaxed and picturesque style being particularly suitable for today's outdoor living, the Federation house continues to delight and attract, thereby creating a need for Federation style leadlight designs.

The picturesque effects of an amazing variety of door types, window shapes, turrets and conservatories which include bay, casement, bullseye, horseshoe, oval and many others, became the perfect medium for leadlight as a decorative effect. Becoming universally popular, it was also used in fanlights, sidelights, interior doors and even firescreens and cabinets. Several of the designs in this book are inspired by and extensions of original Federation works which have come into the studio for repairs or restoration*. The passage of time has made attempts to attribute design source futile - our apologies to the unknown artists of yesteryear!

Early Federation was characterised by the use of square, textured, multicoloured glass panes, plus the use of patriotic motives of Australian flora and fauna, with the sunburst motif symbolising the beginning of the new century and the spirit of a new nation.

The sinuous tendrils and stylised flower shapes of Art Nouveau were an ideal compliment to Federation architecture and started to make their appearance around the turn of the century.

Movement toward simpler forms and detail was noticeable from about 1910 onward, with formal Art Nouveau being indicative of the late Federation era.

The vitality and sparkle of the Federation stained glass was facilitated by the great variety of clear and coloured textured glass used.

The design in Decorating with Australian Federation Stained Glass contrive to give an example from each era, with the emphasis being on the Art Nouveau influence.

JILLIAN SAWYER

PO Box 522
Cannington
Western Australia 6107
Email: firebird@iinet.net.au

Extending

a

Theme

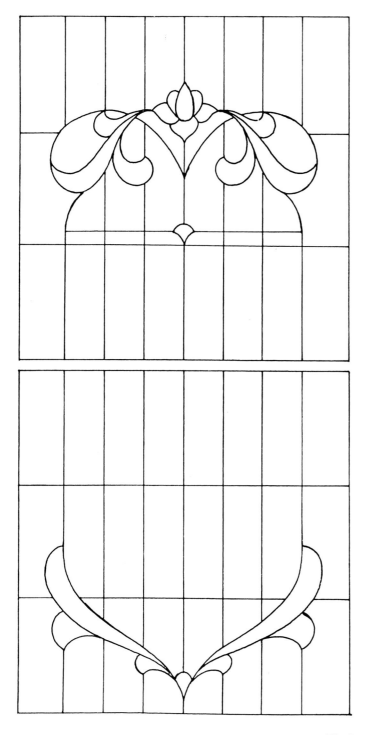

Fig.2

A wonderful example of the effect of decorating with stained glass is illustrated by the residence of Mr and Mrs McOnie.

After having their front door set done (figure 1), the McOnies approached us to design a window for their dining room (figure 2). This window was so pleasing that the use of stained glass was a major consideration in the planning when they decided to extend.

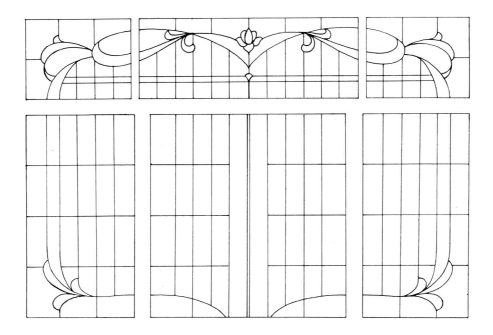

And so from one window an entire extension was co-ordinated including sash windows, French doors and lampshades, with hilites and cupboard doors in the kitchen. The stunning results culminated with this residence being used as a feature in this book.

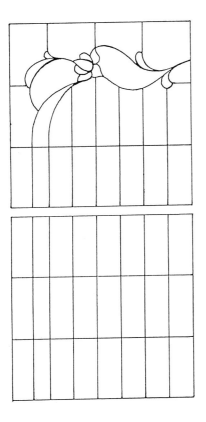 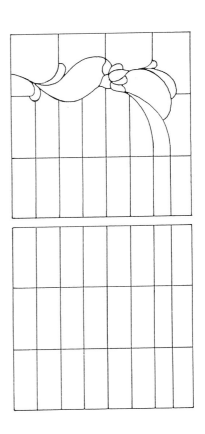

Fig.1

The design for this door set was reconstructed from one surviving original panel from a gracious old home in Narrogin.

HOLLINGSWORTH RESIDENCE

This window was designed to match and compliment the original existing Federation door surround (figure 3).

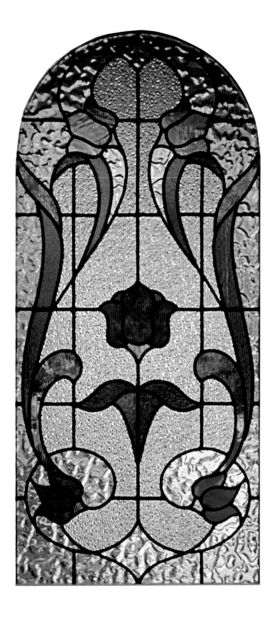

Fig.3

SUTTON RESIDENCE

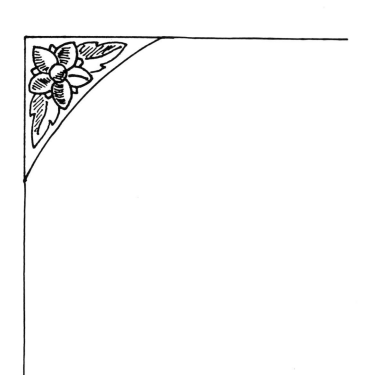

Inspirations
and
Variations

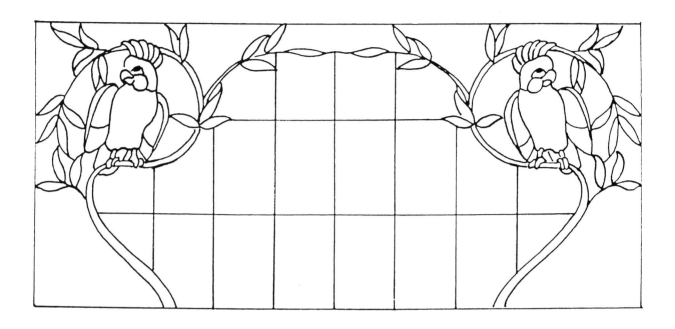

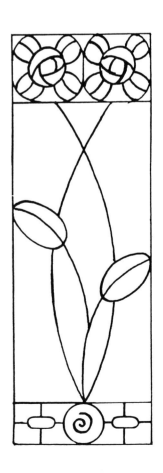

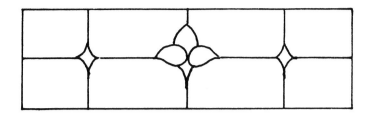

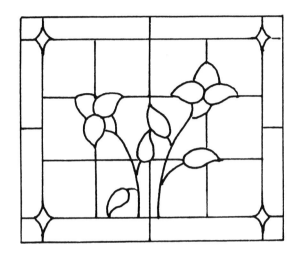

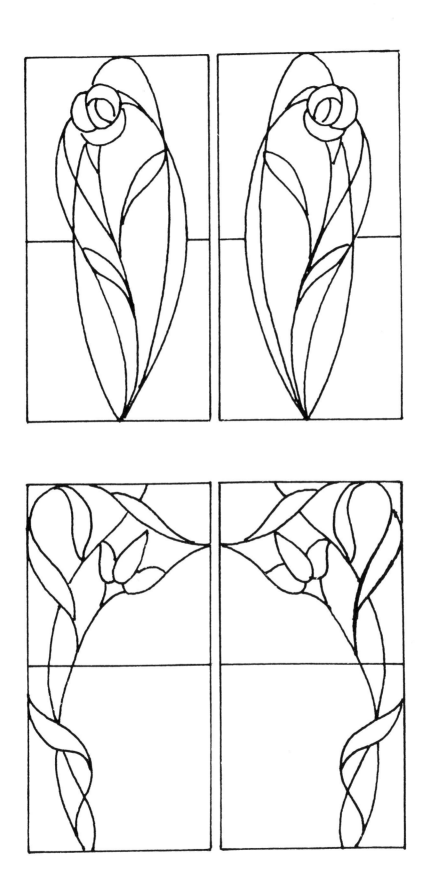

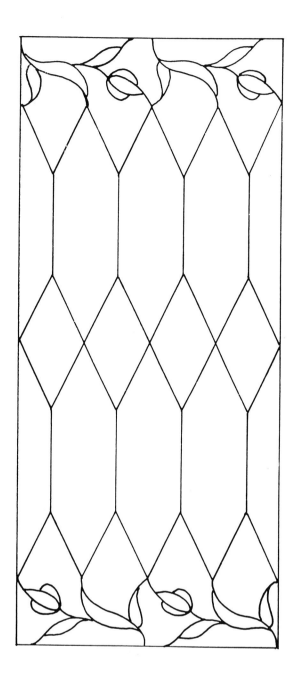

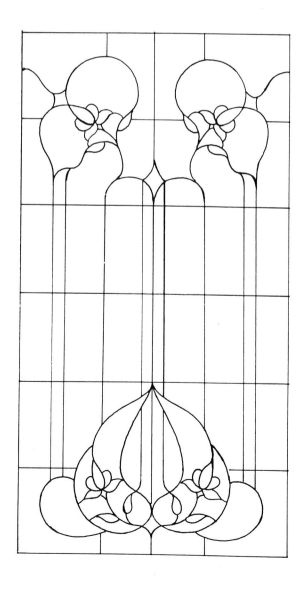

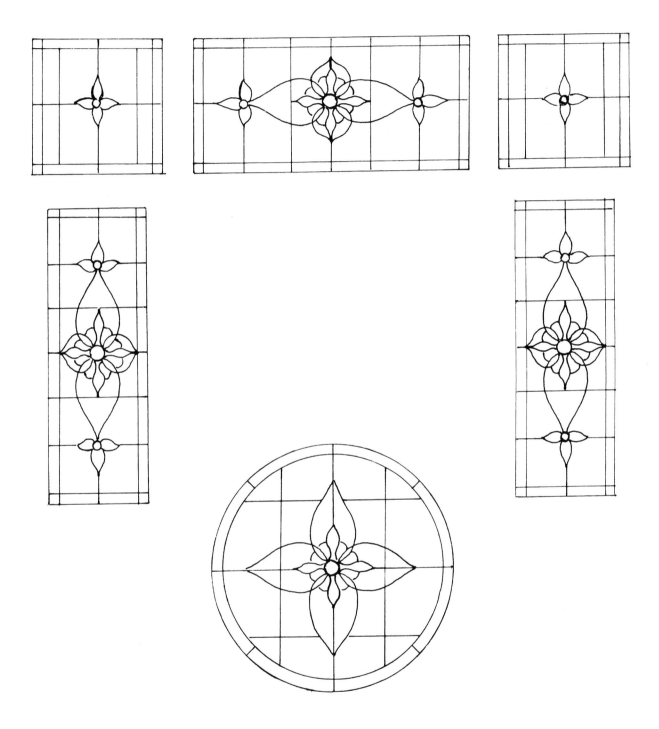

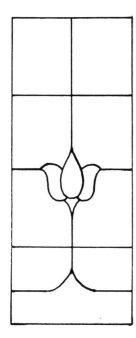

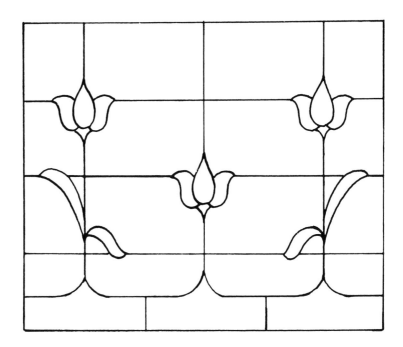

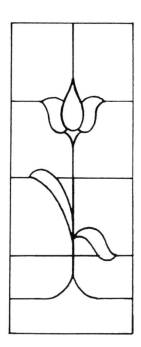

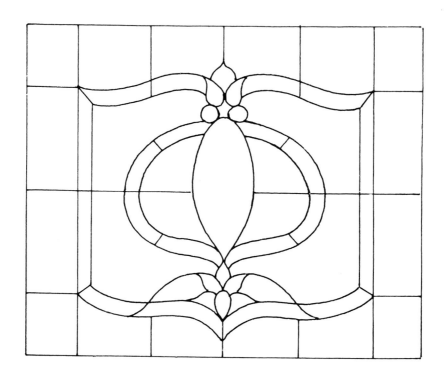

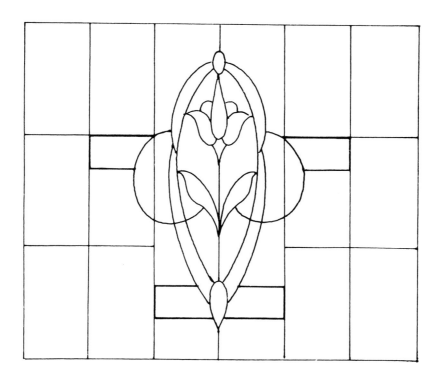

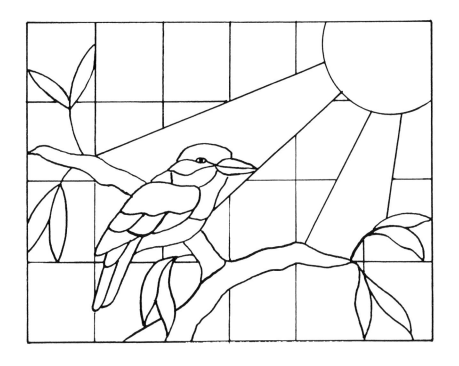

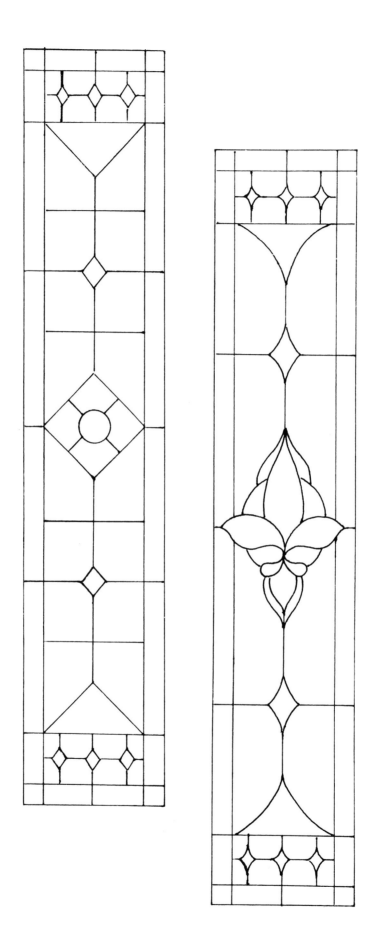

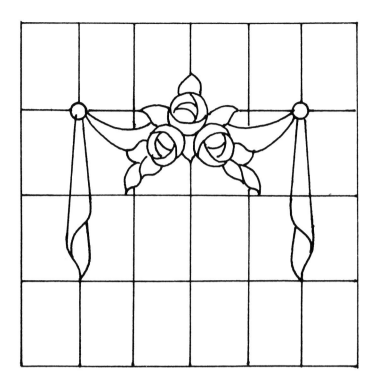

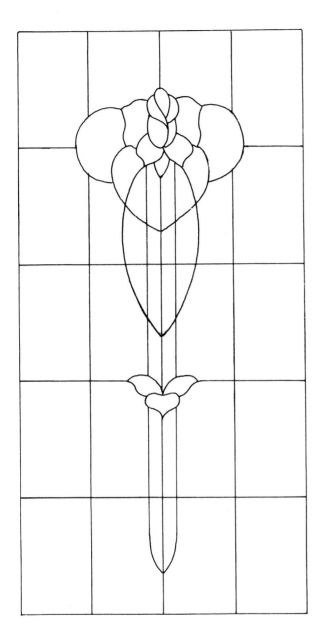

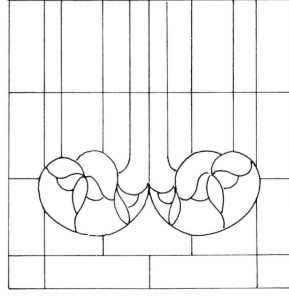

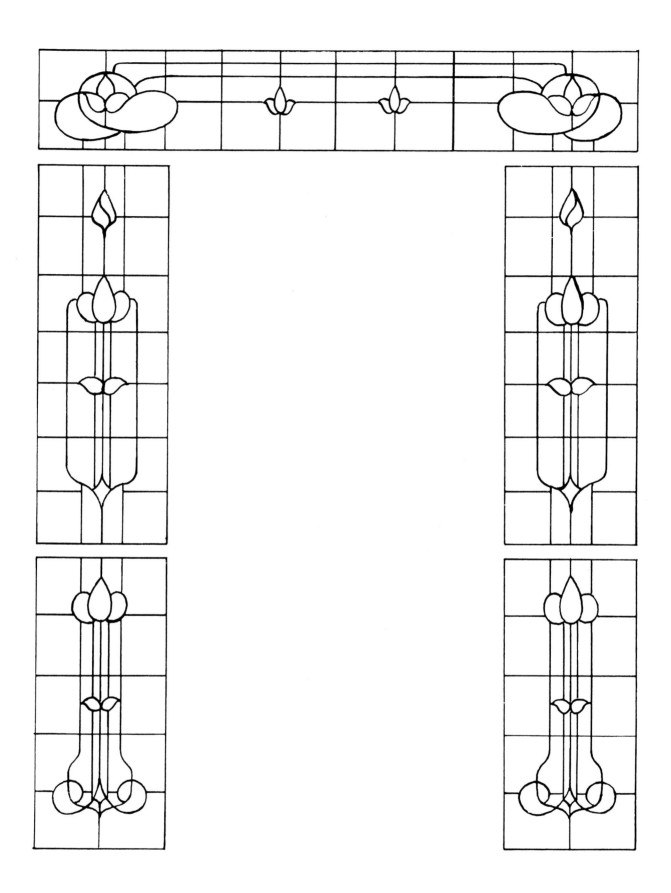

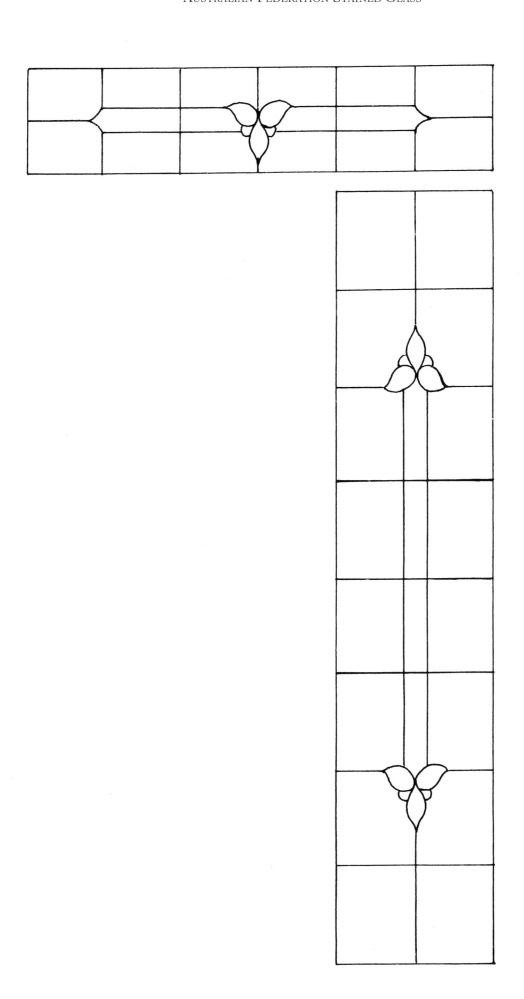

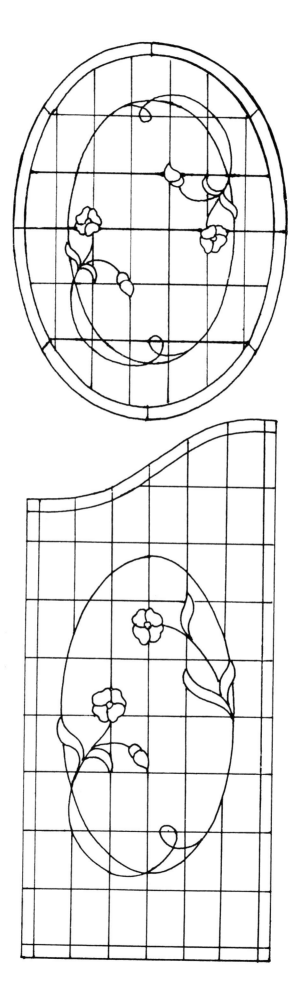

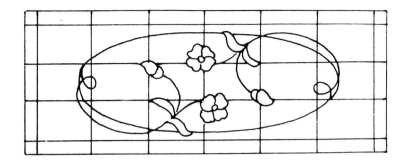

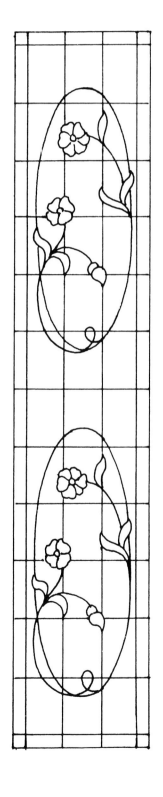
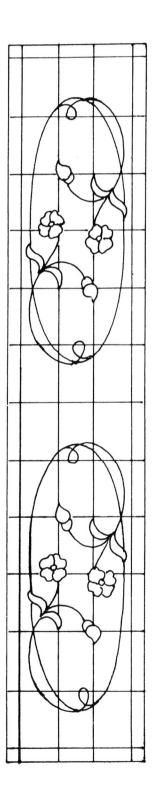

Situations

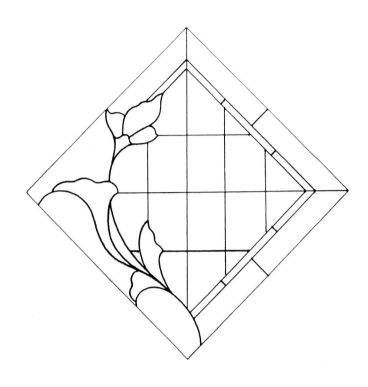

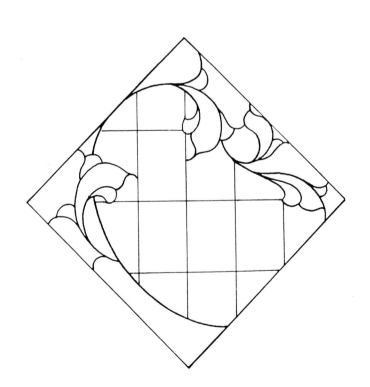

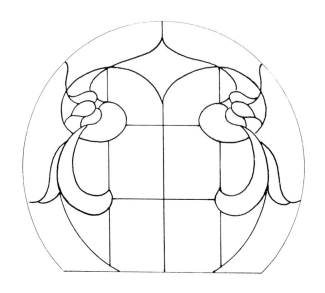

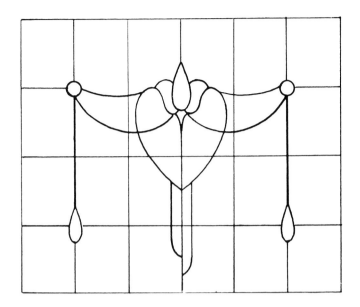

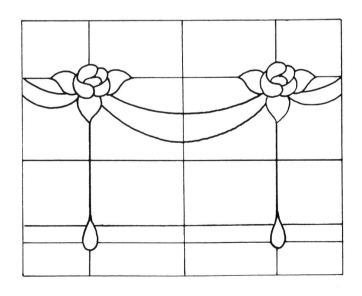

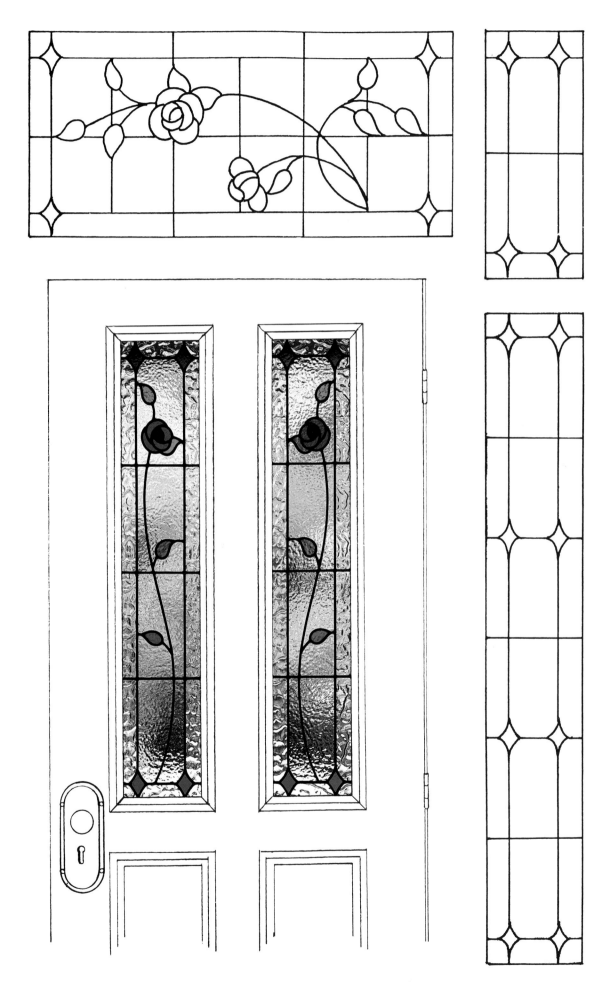

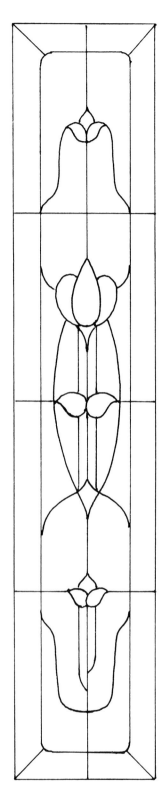

STRAUTIN'S RESIDENCE
(this page and facing page)

NEGOESCU RESIDENCE

This delightful house has almost the full range of Federation window treatments to display with the bullseye and door surround forming the entrance foyer. There are three different examples of bay windows, each consisting of six windows. The floral Art Nouveau theme from the foyer was continued through to these windows, depicting roses, poppies and lillies.

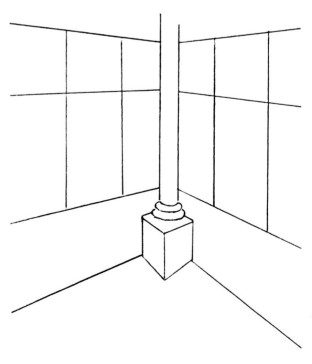

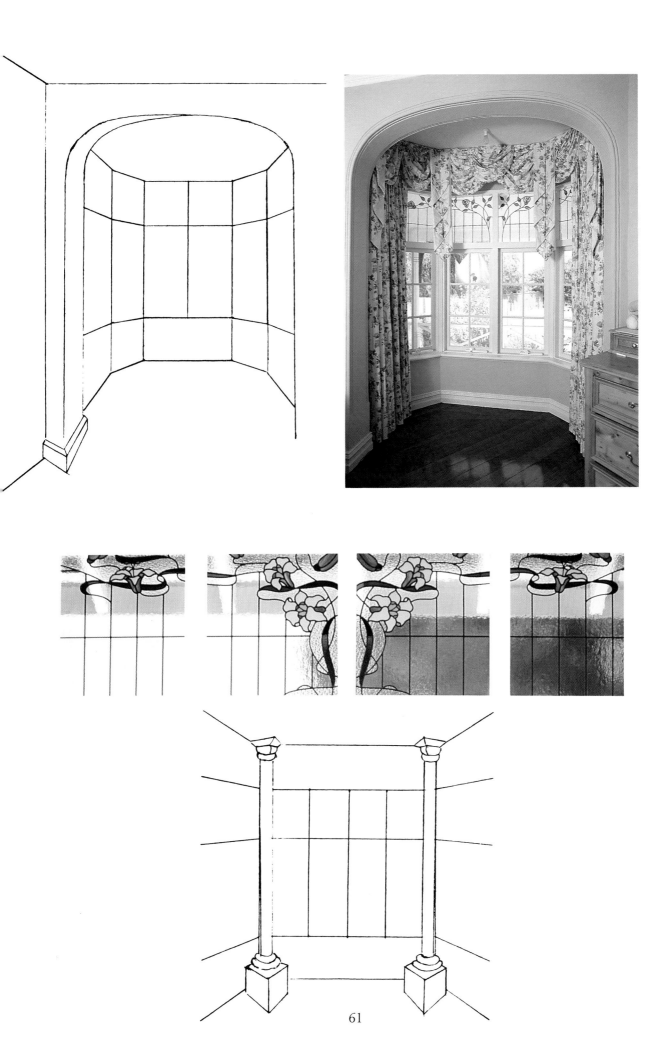

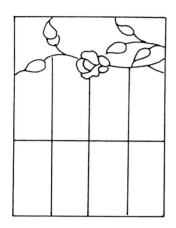
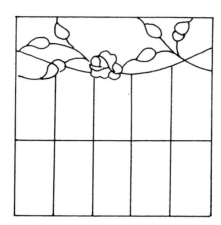

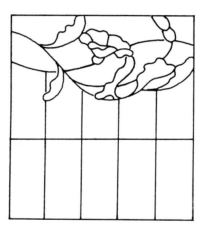

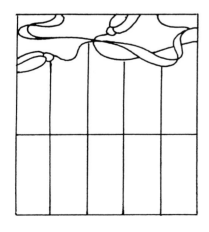
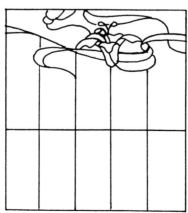

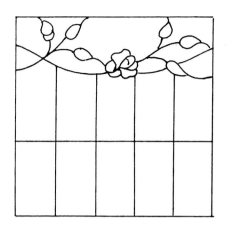
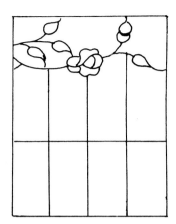

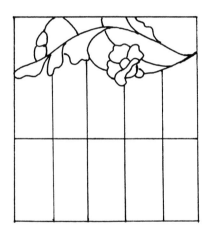
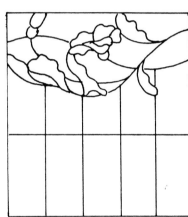
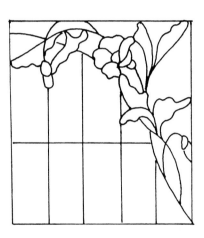

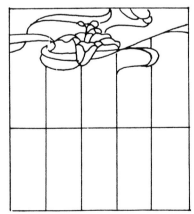
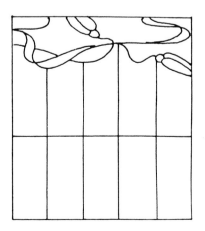

PANTALL RESIDENCE
(see also back cover)